Bookkeeping and Accounting for Beginners

Bookkeeping and Accounting Basics for Small Business Owners

By D.K. Livingston

I0504483

Disclaimer:

The views expressed within this book are those of the author alone. The information contained within this book is based on the opinions, experiences, and observations of the author and is provided "AS-IS". No warranties of any kind are made. Neither the author nor publisher are engaged in rendering professional services of any kind. Neither the author nor publisher will assume liability or responsibility for any loss or damage related directly or indirectly to the information contained within this book.

The author has attempted to be as accurate as possible with the information contained within this book. Neither the author nor publisher will assume responsibility or liability for any errors, omissions, inconsistencies, or inaccuracies.

Table of Contents

Introduction 1
Differences and Similarities Between Accounting and Bookkeeping 3
Differences Between For-Profit and Nonprofit 6
Double-Entry Bookkeeping and Accounting 8
Debits and Credits 8
Exercise 8
Answer Key 9
Income Statement 11
Revenue 11
Expenses 12
Net Profit and Loss 12
How to Fill Out an Income Statement 12
Balance Sheet 14
Formula... 14
Assets... 15
Liabilities... 16
Owner's Equity 18
Cash Flow Statement 19
Operating Activities... 19
Investing Activities.. 20
Financing Activities... 20
Illustration of a Cash Flow Statement 20
Statement of Stockholders' (Shareholders') Equity 23
How to Calculate Earnings Per Share.................................... 24
How to Reconcile a Bank Statement 25
Nonprofit 26
Statement of Activities 26
Statement of Financial Position.. 27
Notes to the Financial Statements 29
Statement of Functional Expenses.. 29
How to Get Started with Virtual Bookkeeping 31
Closing.. 33

Introduction

Doing your own accounting can save you money and give you the peace of mind that the job is getting done right. But you need to know what you're doing.

It can be challenging to maintain accurate bookkeeping records.

There are different things that business owners need to know, such as:

- How to balance the books

- How to keep track of expenses and other transactions

- Tax laws

- Financial statements

Accounting helps users make well-informed economic decisions, while bookkeeping provides a solid basis for the accountant to work with.

Although the fields of bookkeeping and accounting have been practiced for many years, they have undergone changes in the way they are operated.

With the implementation of new technologies, these changes should be expected to continue.

Bookkeeping and accounting can be complex, but they don't have to be scary. This book will break down the different aspects of these two branches and provide guidance on how to effectively perform the tasks that come with them.

Here are some of the topics that will be covered:

• **Double-Entry Bookkeeping and Accounting**

• **How to fill out an Income Statement**

• **Balance Sheet**

• **Cash Flow Statement**

• **How to calculate earnings per share**

• **How to reconcile a bank statement**

• **Nonprofit accounting**

• **How to get started with virtual bookkeeping**

• **and more**

Differences and Similarities Between Accounting and Bookkeeping

Although bookkeeping and accounting are similar in certain ways, they are not entirely the same. Essentially, they are two separate branches in the same field.

Since they are closely related to each other, it is important for every accountant to have at least a basic understanding of bookkeeping, just as it is important for every bookkeeper to have at least a basic understanding of accounting.

Similarities Between Accounting and Bookkeeping

• Both of them deal with financial data

• Both of them involve the generation and classification of reports by the utilization of financial transactions

Differences Between Accounting and Bookkeeping

Skills:

Accounting- Requires special skills

Bookkeeping- No special skills are required

Complexity:

Accounting- Fairly complex and requires analysis

Bookkeeping – More straightforward than accounting and does not require analysis

Roles:

Accounting-

• Verification and analysis of data

• Generation of reports through the use of the data that was verified and analyzed

• Performance of audits

• Preparation of tax returns, balance sheets, and income statements

Bookkeeping-

• Recording of financial transactions

• Production of invoices

• Completion of payroll

• Posting of debits and credits

• Maintenance and balancing of historical accounts, subsidiaries, and ledgers

Primary Goal:

Accounting- The primary goal of accounting is to identify the financial situation and turn data into information

Bookkeeping- The primary goal of bookkeeping is to generate data about a company's activities and to make sure that the records of the financial transactions are accurate

Financial Statements:

Accounting- Involves the preparation of financial statements

Bookkeeping- Does not involve the preparation of financial statements

Decisions:

Accounting- The accountant makes decisions

Bookkeeping- The bookkeeper carries out the accountant's decisions

If you are an entrepreneur who would like to handle all of the financial situations by yourself, you will need to take on the role of accountant and bookkeeper, which is why this book will include information on both.

Differences Between For-Profit and Nonprofit

Before you begin the accounting and bookkeeping process for your business, it's important to be clear as to whether your company is nonprofit of for-profit.

Nonprofit organizations have a primary objective of serving communities. Their secondary objective is to generate enough revenue to continue carrying out their operations.

For-profit organizations are run with the intention of generating profits for the business owners. Their secondary objective is to provide services or products.

To stay in business, nonprofit organizations often rely on contributions. An example would be a church relying on the churchgoer's tithes and offering.

Other nonprofit organizations rely on membership dues, fundraising, public and private grants, income from investments, etc.

Here is a breakdown of the differences between nonprofits and for-profits:

Ownership:

Nonprofits- No owners

For-Profits- Owned by stockholders

Primary Objective:

Nonprofit- Offer products or services to people

6

For-Profit- Generate profits

Taxes (at least in the U.S.):

Nonprofit- Can be considered exempt from income tax if approved by the IRS

For-Profit- Required to pay income tax if the business is profitable enough

Revenue Generation:

Nonprofit- Typically comes from donations, membership fees or dues, fundraising, grants, and income from investments

For-Profit- Typically comes from product sales, investment gains, fees that are charged for services, and income from investments

Asset Type:

Nonprofit- Net assets

For-Profit- Equity from stockholders

Statements issued:

Nonprofit- Statement of Activities, Statement of Financial Position, Statement of Functional Expenses, Statement of Cash flow, and Notes to Financial Statements

For-Profit- Income Statement, Balance Sheet, Statement of Cash Flow, Statement of Stockholders' Equity, and Notes to Financial Statements

For additional information on tax-related situations, visit irs.gov

Double-Entry Bookkeeping and Accounting

F or the most part, single-entry bookkeeping is a method of the past. Currently, most companies opt for the double-entry method, which involves two accounts for every transaction.

Debits and Credits

In double-entry bookkeeping, each one of the accounts will have two sides—debit and credit. Debiting an asset will *in*crease it, and crediting an asset will *de*crease it.

On the account, debits will be displayed on the left side; credits will be displayed on the right side.

Exercise

To practice an exercise, suppose a company that started with no money went on to borrow $50,000, before spending $10,000 on rental property and acquiring $5,000 in sales from customers.

Copy down the ledger example below in your mind or on a piece of paper, and see if you can fill in the blanks. Which numbers from the above example should go into which debit and credit columns?

The answer key will be below the exercise.

DebitCredit

Cash

J.H. Washington, capital

Rental Property

Cash

Cash

Product Sales Revenue

Tip: The amount in the Credit column must match the amount in the Debit column for each transaction.

Answer Key

Cash: $50,000 in the Debit column.

J.H. Washington, capital: $50,000 in the Credit column.

Rental Property: $10,000 in the Debit column.

Cash: $10,000 in the Credit column.

Cash: $5,000 in the Debit column.

Product Sales Revenue: $5,000 in the Credit column.

Try practicing by using your own examples that fit your needs. For instance, if your business is blogging, instead of using Rental Property in the exercise, you might want to use computer supplies, office space utilities, etc.

Income Statement

An income statement is a statement that is used for the purpose of reporting the financial performance of a business over a certain time frame.

It is also referred to as the Profit and Loss Statement or the Statement of Revenue and Expense.

For-Profit businesses are required to send income statements to the SEC (Securities and Exchange Commission).

The income statement is generally composed of:

- **Revenue**

- **Expenses**

- **Net profit**

- **Loss**

Revenue

Revenue can be split into two different branches—Operating Revenue and Non-Operating Revenue.

Operating Revenue is realized via primary activities, while Non-Operating Revenue is realized via secondary activities.

Examples of Operating Revenue would be the sale of a product or income generated through a provided service.

Examples of Non-Operating Revenue would be rental income, money from the business that was placed in the bank and earned interest, and royalty payments.

Note: Revenue should be recorded when it is earned, not when it was received.

Expenses

Expenses can be grouped into two categories—Primary Activity Expenses and Secondary Activity Expenses.

Primary Activity Expenses are the expenses that come about from operating revenue that is connected to the primary activities of the company. This can include depreciation, sales commissions or wages that are paid out to employees, utility costs, and the cost of goods sold.

Secondary Activity Expenses are the expenses that are connected to secondary business activities, such as interest that was paid on money that was loaned to the company.

Net Profit and Loss

The profit or loss is calculated by adding up all of the revenue streams and deducting all of the expenses (primary and secondary expenses).

How to Fill Out an Income Statement

When filling out an income statement, the information should be broken down and presented in a readable manner.

To illustrate, an income statement that is broken down in a presentable manner might look like this:

Revenue_____

Cost of Goods Sold_____

Gross Profit_____

Expenses

Administrative Expenses_____

Depreciation Expenses_____

Marketing Expenses_____

Interest_____

Other Expenses_____

Total Expenses_____

Profit Before Tax_____

Income statement templates can be used and inputted into a program, such as, *Excel*.

Balance Sheet

Another important financial statement is the balance sheet. The purpose of a balance sheet is to report a company's assets, shareholder's equity, and liabilities over a specified time frame. This allows creditors and other people to view what a business owns and owes to other parties.

The balance sheet is split into two different sections:

• **Assets**

• **Liabilities and Shareholder's Equity**

Formula

The formula for a balance sheet is based on the fundamental equation of:

Assets = Liabilities + Owner's Equity

To illustrate, if Jack acquires property that costs $500,000, then uses $100,000 as a down payment, he will still owe $400,000 for the mortgage. This means Jack would have $100,000 of equity on the property.

Following the formula, Jack's situation would look like this:

$500,000 (Assets) = $400,000 (Liabilities) + $100,000 (Owner's Equity)

The point of a financial statement, including the balance sheet, is to track financial numbers over a period of time. For this reason, it's good to get accustomed to the change in statistics that will inevitably accompany the change in time.

Following the same example, this is what Jack's situation might look like a year later, after he pays off an additional $50,000 for the property:

$500,000 (Assets) = $350,000 (Liabilities) + $150,000 (Owner's Equity)

Since Jack made progress with his mortgage payments, his liabilities decreased and his Equity increased.

This is why it's important to update balance sheets from time to time. As time progresses, financial numbers tend to change.

The more assets and liabilities a company has, the more complex the balance sheet will get.

Assets

An asset is something of value that benefits a person or company in some way. It could be a resource or something a person or company owns.

Some examples of assets include:

• Accounts

• Cash and cash equivalents

• Inventory

• Property

• Long-term investments

In financial accounting, assets can be split into two groups—Current and Long-term.

Current Assets

Current assets are assets that are anticipated to be transformed into cash or used within the course of a year or in the cycle of operation, whichever comes first.

If an asset interferes with the normal operations of the company, it should not be considered a current asset.

There are five major categories that are included in the *Current Assets* section:

- Cash and cash equivalents

- Inventory

- Prepaid expenses

- Receivables

- Short-term investments

Long-term Assets

If assets are not expected to be used or converted to cash within twelve months, they are typically considered to be *Long-term Assets*.

This can often include:

- Stocks and bonds that are held long-term

- Property or land that is held long-term

- Pension funds

Liabilities

In accounting, a liability is essentially money that a business owes, customer deposits or customer prepayments in which a business has not yet earned, a situation that can result in a transfer or utilization of assets, or any kind of obligation that would require the business to lose money.

Here are some examples:

• Wages that need to be paid to employees

• Paying income taxes

• Paying interest

Liabilities can be grouped into two groups—Current and Long-term.

Current Liabilities

This type of liability occurs when a company's obligations are due within twelve months of the balance sheet date or within the operating cycle, whichever occurs first.

Some examples include:

• Accounts

• Accounts payable

• Income Taxes

• Portion of long-term loans that are anticipated to be liquidated within a year

• Unearned revenue

• Wages

Long-term Liabilities

These are liabilities that are *not* anticipated to be liquidated within a year.

These can include:

• Long-term bonds issued

- Long-term leases

- Long-term product warranties

- Notes payable

- Pension obligations

Owner's Equity

In accounting, owner's equity is made up of the net assets of an entity. A net asset is the difference between total assets and total liabilities.

The types of accounts that make up the owner's equity can include:

- Capital surplus

- Preferred stock

- Reserve

- Retained earnings

- Share capital

- Stock options

Cash Flow Statement

The cash flow statement—also referred to as *Statement of Cash Flows*—is one of the core financial statements. It reports the cash that has gone in (cash inflow) and out (cash outflow) of a business.

The main cash flows that occur within a certain time frame are reported under three sections:

- **Operating activities**

- **Investing activities**

- **Financing activities**

Operating Activities

Operating activities are the main cash-producing activities of the business. This generally includes cash flows that are related to sales and purchases.

The operating activities can be presented by using what is known as the *Direct* method or the *Indirect* method.

The *Indirect* method, which is more commonly used among corporations than the *Direct* method, presents the operational cash flows as a reconciliation from profit to cash flow to make sure that the cash going out of the account lines up with the money that was actually spent.

The *Direct* method presents the operational cash flows as cash coming in from sales and cash going out from expenses.

Investing Activities

The next portion of the Cash Flow Statement is used for the purpose of reporting the cash outflows that are related to the acquiring of non-current assets and the cash inflows received from the sale of non-current assets.

This typically includes property, plant, equipment, and other non-current assets that were obtained during the accounting time frame.

Financing Activities

The third portion of the Cash Flow Statement serves the purpose of reporting the cash that was received when the business borrowed capital or issued securities.

This can include the payment of a dividend, the borrowing and repayment of loans, and issuing and buying back shares of stocks or bonds.

Illustration of a Cash Flow Statement

Here is an example of what the layout might look like for a Cash Flow Statement:

Year Ended December 31,

Operating Activities:

Net income

Adjustments to reconcile net income to net cash from operating activities:

Depreciation of property, equipment, and other amortization_____

Other operating expense, net_____

Other expense (income), net_____

Changes in operating assets and liabilities:

Accounts receivable, net and other_____

Accounts payable_____

Accrued expenses and other_____

Unearned revenue_____

Net cash provided from operating activities_____

Investing Activities:

Purchases of property and equipment_____

Proceeds from sale of property_____

Sale of securities_____

Purchases of securities_____

Net cash used in investing activities_____

Financing Activities:

Proceeds from long-term debt and other_____

Repayments of long-term debt and other_____

Cash dividends_____

Principal repayments of capital lease obligations_____

Principal repayments of finance lease obligations_____

Net cash provided by financing activities_____

Net increase in cash and cash equivalents_____

Cash and cash equivalents and end of year_____

Statement of Stockholders' (Shareholders') Equity

This is the financial statement that includes the balances of stockholders' equity and the changes that occurred within it over a specified time frame.

The statement features the beginning balance for each portion of equity, additions to and subtractions from the beginning balances, and the ending balances that result from the additions and subtractions.

The different columns in the grid-like statement could include:

• Accumulated and other comprehensive income

• Common stock

• Preferred stock

• Retained earnings

• Treasury stock

How to Calculate Earnings Per Share

E arnings per share is the calculation that displays how profitable a business is when it comes to shareholders. It is often used to gain insight into the financial health of a company.

A higher earnings per share typically indicates that a business is profitable to the point that it can afford to pay out additional money to its shareholders, often in the form of increased dividends.

The formula for calculating earnings per share is:

Net income – preferred dividends / average outstanding common shares

Illustration:

Net income: $100,000,000

Preferred Dividends: $20,000,000

Average number of outstanding common shares: 2,000,000

$100,000,000 - $20,000,000 / 2,000,000 = **$40 earnings per share**

How to Reconcile a Bank Statement

Reconciling a bank statement involves the comparison of the numbers on the bank statement and the numbers on the company's general ledger account, and then figuring out why the numbers don't match.

The process is similar to balancing a personal checkbook.

When determining why the numbers don't match, consider the following reasons:

• Bank fees and other charges that you have forgotten or were not aware of

• Check image fees or printing charges

• Checks that were written but not yet cleared

• Company receipts that have not yet been deposited in the bank

• Bank rejecting a check that you thought was accepted

If these things are all taken into consideration and have been successfully accounted for and the issue still remains, make sure you recheck the amounts entered in the general ledger and verify that the information was entered correctly.

Nonprofit

As stated earlier in the book, nonprofit organizations have a primary objective of serving communities. Their secondary objective is to generate enough revenue to continue carrying out their operations.

This section will go into more detail about the various aspects of non-profit accounting.

Note: Statement of Cash Flow, which is also a part of nonprofit accounting, generally involves the same concepts mentioned in the *Cash Flow Statement* chapter, so it will not be included in this chapter.

Statement of Activities

Instead of using an income statement, nonprofit organizations use a statement of activities, which reports revenue and amounts of expenses.

Here is what a Statement of Activities might look like:

Revenues

Contributions_____

Investment Income_____

Net assets released from restrictions_____

Total revenues, gains, and other support_____

Expenses

General administration_____

Program services_____

Fundraising_____

Total expenses_____

Change in net assets_____

+ Net assets – beginning_____

= Net assets – ending_____

Statement of Financial Position

This is what nonprofits use instead of using a balance sheet. A Statement of Financial Position is used to report the nonprofit organization's assets and liabilities.

Utilizing the formula of *Assets = Liabilities + Net Assets*, a person that donates $100 to an organization should display on the nonprofit's statement as:

Assets

+ $100

= Liabilities

Net Assets

+ $100

Utilizing the same formula, a nonprofit organization that spends $50 for equipment that will be used right away should display on the statement as:

Assets

-$50

= Liabilities

Net Assets

-$50

Here is what a Statement of Financial Position might look like:

Assets

Current Assets

Cash and Cash Equivalents_____

Inventory_____

Total Current Assets_____

Fixed Assets

Accumulated Depreciation_____

Total Fixed Assets_____

Other Assets

Accumulated Amortization

Total Other Assets_____

Total Assets_____

Liabilities

Current Liabilities

Accounts Payable_____

Accrued Expenses_____

Total Current Liabilities_____

Long-term Liabilities_____

Total Liabilities_____

Notes to the Financial Statements

Notes to the Financial Statements provide specific details to the organization's liquidity, restrictions, etc.

Statement of Financial Position and Statement of Activities provide a more generalized version of the organization's finances.

Donors, creditors, and others usually find such statements to be substantial, as listing all of the individual expenses on a statement can be very time consuming.

For example, instead of summarizing the total expenses for office supplies and listing the overall expense under the category of "Equipment", the Notes to the Financial Statement might include the cost for each box of pens, each pack of stationary, each box of ink cartridges for the printer, etc.

But for anyone who might want more specific details, Notes to the Financial Statement can be useful.

Statement of Functional Expenses

This statement reports expenses by their function and by the type of expenses.

Reported expenses by their function can include management, fundraising, etc. Reported expenses by the type of expense can include salaries, utilities, etc.

When filling out the Statement of Functional Expenses, the diagram can display the function of expenses across the top of the chart. The type of the expenses can be displayed on the left side of the chart from top to bottom.

To illustrate:

	Management	Fundraising	Total
Salaries			
Utilities			
Supplies			
Depreciation			
Total			

How to Get Started with Virtual Bookkeeping

The low startup costs and the potential to make a living can make starting your own virtual bookkeeping business a desirable choice.

Remote bookkeeping jobs can be found by regularly checking on indeed.com

It can also help to set up a freelance website, which can allow you to efficiently place your portfolio, resume, and pay rates all in one convenient place.

Before reaching out to clients, it's important to establish yourself as a Limited Liability Company (LLC). This will help protect your business from personal liability while you handle the money of other people. Be aware that registering as a company does involve fees that can vary from state to state.

In addition to registering your business as a LLC, you might want to get insurance for your company, as well.

Find a niche (or multiple niches) that you are interested in, and then pursue them. Many different types of companies hire bookkeepers, so it makes sense to stick with the ones that you will be the most passionate about.

As you market yourself and fill out your resume, don't forget to mention that you will keep the private and personal information of your clients secure, and of course, make sure you follow through on that.

Explain how you plan to keep their information secure. Perhaps you have a filing cabinet with locking drawers that you plan to keep their paperwork in. Or maybe you have a security system in your home office.

Have a password-protected computer account that only you know the password to.

You will also need to select bookkeeping software.

As far as deciding on a fee structure, try to be realistic and stay within the low to median range of your competitors if you are just starting out. Fees can be increased later on after you've gained enough experience in your business to warrant that.

<u>Closing</u>

Bookkeeping and accounting have their differences, but they both go hand in hand. They can both help business owners manage their companies more efficiently.

Using the books can help you determine what works best for a company and what does not.

Keeping track of expenses and identifying financial errors can help a business become more profitable.

Bookkeeping and accounting each have their own individual uses, and in order to gain a bigger perspective of a company's financial picture, it's good to utilize both.

www.ingramcontent.com/pod-product-compliance
Lightning Source LLC
Chambersburg PA
CBHW030543220526
45463CB00007B/2959